THE
PATH
BETWEEN
US

STUDY GUIDE

SIX SESSIONS

SUZANNE STABILE

IVP Books
An imprint of InterVarsity Press
Downers Grove, Illinois

InterVarsity Press
P.O. Box 1400, Downers Grove, IL 60515-1426
ivpress.com
email@ivpress.com

©2018 by Suzanne Stabile

InterVarsity Press® is the book-publishing division of InterVarsity Christian Fellowship/USA®, a movement of students and faculty active on campus at hundreds of universities, colleges, and schools of nursing in the United States of America, and a member movement of the International Fellowship of Evangelical Students. For information about local and regional activities, visit intervarsity.org.

All Scripture quotations, unless otherwise indicated, are taken from The Holy Bible, New International Version®, NIV®. Copyright © 1973, 1978, 1984, 2011 by Biblica, Inc.™ Used by permission of Zondervan. All rights reserved worldwide. www.zondervan.com. The "NIV" and "New International Version" are trademarks registered in the United States Patent and Trademark Office by Biblica, Inc.™

Cover design: David Fassett
Interior design: Daniel van Loon
Images: people walking: © Ricardo Dias / EyeEm / Getty Images
wavy line background: © Kalisson / iStock / Getty Images
Author photo: Courtney Perry

ISBN 978-0-8308-4643-6 (print)
ISBN 978-0-8308-8646-3 (digital)

Printed in the United States of America ♾

P 21 20 19 18 17 16 15 14 13 12 11 10 9 8 7 6

Y 36 35 34 33 32 31 30 29 28 27 26 25 24 23 22 21 20

CONTENTS

INTRODUCTION

Welcome to *The Path Between Us Study Guide*! I am so glad you have decided to go deeper into the wisdom of the Enneagram. This ancient resource has much to offer as we seek to understand ourselves and those around us more fully. As we gain an appreciation for the gifts each of us brings to the table, along with the limitations and problems that are associated with each of the nine numbers, we are capable of offering ourselves, and the world, far more compassion. That offering is a gift for everyone.

Over the next six sessions, this study guide will focus on how each of us can grow and mature in the ways we relate to one another. While it's never wise to guess at or assign Enneagram numbers to other people, we can honor the differences between us and the people we love by learning about the other eight Enneagram numbers. Keep in mind that in Enneagram understanding, your greatest strength is also your greatest weakness. It's likely that the way you are in the world—for example, the way you communicate or how you react when you're excited—is different from your siblings, colleagues, and friends.

Each session will focus on a different *topic* rather than an Enneagram number. This means it will be helpful to have read *The Path Between Us* before you begin your journey through this study guide since it doesn't follow the same chapter structure as the book. And you'll probably find it helpful to refer to the book periodically as you journey from week to week.

It is also worth noting here that if all of this talk of Enneagram numbers isn't making much sense to you, now would be a good time to pause and read (or re-read!) *The Road Back to You: An Enneagram Journey to Self-Discovery*. That book is designed to help you identify your own Enneagram number and to give a brief overview of the other eight numbers. It will be important for ongoing Enneagram work that you have a good handle on the basics of your own number.

Because *The Path Between Us* explores the wisdom the Enneagram offers in helping us grow relationally, you might find it most helpful to do this study in a group. The content here is designed for groups of all sizes: a gathering in a home or at your church, or just three of you at your favorite coffee shop. (Of course, even if you decide to go through this study alone, there is still much wisdom to be gleaned.)

For any group, there are certain ground rules that will make the time together most productive and valuable for everyone.

- *Make this group a priority.* Make every effort to be here each week, to come on time, and to set your phone aside so you won't be interrupted. Each session is designed to last about ninety minutes, so make space in your life to be fully present for that window of time each week.

- *Listen. Then listen again.* As with any self-reflective work, when we discover new wisdom in the Enneagram, we are often eager to share with others what we are learning. Pay close attention to whether you are listening closely to others with the same enthusiasm you have for sharing your own epiphanies. This doesn't mean you should shut down—often the thing you have learned is the very thing someone else in the group needs to hear—but it does mean that on balance, you should be listening more than you are speaking.

■ *Be willing to take a risk.* Depending on how well you know the others in your group, responding to some or all of these questions will require vulnerability. Often it is when we're honest that we can truly learn from one another, so consider making the decision to take some risks as you work through this study.

■ *Make this a safe space.* Other people's stories are precisely that—their stories. Some people will be sharing particularly vulnerable parts of themselves in this group. Please respect their privacy and honor their trust by not disclosing their personal stories and concerns to anyone outside the group.

I'm so thankful you're here. The Enneagram has been so helpful in my life. It offers me compassion for myself and for others, wisdom in making space for people who don't see the world the way I do, and grace for the strangers I encounter along the way. Know that you have my prayers and best wishes as we all continue to work toward creating a world that offers more compassion and more peace as we walk beside one another on the journey.

THE BEST PART OF YOU IS THE WORST PART OF YOU

*The truth is that all relationships
are messy and unpredictable.*

THE PATH BETWEEN US

*W*elcome! In this first session, we will begin to get to know one another and explore the truth that each number's greatest strength can also be a potentially damaging weakness.

We will start by naming the numbers of the people in our group and listing other people we know who have identified their Enneagram type and shared it with us. There is a tendency to want to assign numbers to people in our lives who don't yet know the Enneagram. That is seldom, if ever, beneficial. Your Enneagram number is not determined by your behavior—it depends almost entirely on your motivation for doing what you do, and that is difficult, if not impossible, for others to know.

If you are using this study guide and you're not in a group, then the best way for you to proceed would be to commit to looking at yourself in relation to what you have learned about every other number from either *The Road Back to You* or *The Path Between Us*.

STRENGTHS AND WEAKNESSES OF OUR NUMBERS

As the Enneagram teaches us, the best part of you is also the worst part of you. Read through "Some of the Best and Worst of Us" to see examples of what this looks like for each number.

SOME *of the* BEST *and* WORST *of* US

1s   **BEST:** Ones have an amazing ability to assess almost everything in terms of how it could be better, and they think it's their responsibility to make people, things, and situations what they could be.

WORST: Ones can often be overly critical of themselves and others. As they go about correcting what is inadequate or wrong, it often leaves others feeling like they can't measure up to the One's high standards.

2s   **BEST:** Twos can easily sense what other people need and are generous in trying to meet those needs.

WORST: Twos have notoriously poor boundaries. When involved in "taking care" of others they don't know how much to give, so they often give too much and then return to their own lives exhausted and unable to tend to their primary responsibilities and their personal needs. The result is often a feeling of being taken for granted, and resentment follows.

3s   **BEST:** Threes set goals for themselves and then they reach them—both short-term and long-term goals. Threes have a strong desire to help others reach their potential, and they enthusiastically share their strategies and experience when asked for help or advice. Added to that, they have both the desire and the ability to be whatever a situation calls for.

WORST: Because Threes are focused on "the goal" they sometimes fail to be mindful of both the feelings and the contributions of others. And because of their ability to shape-shift into what others want them to be, they are sometimes more cynical and suspicious of the rest of us, thinking we can do the same.

4s **BEST:** Fours engage life with a fullness that is unique to their number. They are committed to authenticity, and they are the only number on the Enneagram that can bear witness to pain without having to fix it.

WORST: Fours misunderstand the way other numbers see the world as a lack of interest in them or their thoughts and feelings, and they respond by pulling away. Fours can over-identify with their feelings of sadness or regret, and that intensity can be too much for others.

5s **BEST:** Fives are measured, thoughtful, and self-sufficient. They are good listeners and the only number on the Enneagram that is capable of true neutrality.

WORST: While Fives are good listeners, they don't share much about themselves and their lives with others, which often makes relationships feel one sided. And the other side of the gift of neutrality is that it may be hard for Fives to be passionate about things that are important to those they love.

6s **BEST:** Sixes are steadfast and loyal. Of all the Enneagram numbers, they are the most concerned about the common good, and they are the people who hold together all of the communities that we belong to.

WORST: The passion for Sixes is fear, and they struggle to trust themselves. So they are hesitant to trust their own experience of life and what they have to offer to the communities they belong to. Their anxiety is often a problem in relationships.

7s **BEST:** Sevens are upbeat and optimistic and add joy to the lives of those they are with. They are creative and they believe there is a solution to every problem. And once they are committed to a relationship they are all in.

WORST: Sevens' fear of being trapped in pain keeps them from being willing to show up and address problems. Their fear of doing the same thing over and over again makes it hard for them to settle down with a single-pointed focus and work until a project is complete.

8s **BEST:** Eights are dynamic, creative, and confident leaders. They are unafraid of those who are in authority, and they have a heart for the underdog. They insist that others pursue their own interests and are cheerleaders for others who are willing to give their all and do their best.

WORST: Eights struggle to understand that vulnerability is not weakness, so they don't do well with vulnerability in themselves or in others. And Eights are usually unaware of the effect they have on other people, which is often the source of misunderstanding in relationships.

9s **BEST:** Nines are natural mediators in that they see at least two sides to everything. They are peaceful and are the least controlling number on the Enneagram.

WORST: It is as much a problem as it is a gift that Nines see at least two sides to everything. It makes it very difficult for them to be sure of themselves and the choices they make. And Nines merge with the agendas of others, usually in an effort to avoid conflict. Sometimes avoiding conflict causes conflict.

At the end of the day, none of us really knows what it's like to be in someone else's skin. So feel free to ask questions of your group members about their feelings and experiences.

After reviewing this list, allow each person in your group to answer the following questions:

> You are emotionally vulnerable whether you want to be or not, especially with those you love.

1. Which of the nine numbers do you resonate with most, and why?

2. Have you ever had cause before to realize that the best thing about you may also be the worst thing about you? If so, how did you come to that knowledge?

3. What is a weakness you are aware that you have?

THE CHALLENGE OF CHANGE

The Enneagram teaches us that our number, or our way of seeing the world, was well-honed by the time we were five or six. So we have all been responding to life in predictable, habitual ways since we were children. It's a challenge to change those patterns of behavior. Our tendency is to believe we can do anything if we work hard enough, but that isn't true when talking about personality. Willpower is a myth that is fueled by emotion, and it will not serve you well in dealing with your Enneagram number. You cannot clench your fists or grit your teeth and decisively make changes in your personality.

Two of the best things you can do to make changes that would enhance your relationships involve *self-observation* and *allowing*.

1. Practice observing yourself nonjudgmentally. It won't be easy. But when we judge ourselves, we defend ourselves and then we are deeper in personality than when we started. Just observe your behavior, acknowledge it, and move on.

2. Practice allowing parts of your personality that don't serve you well to simply fall away. Try to avoid feeling frustrated or angry, and after you acknowledge the behavior that you are trying to change just let it go. The result won't be immediate, but after time you will find that a new way of responding to similar situations will emerge.

The following charts will give you some suggestions of things to watch for in your number that may cause problems in your relationships.

ONES, TWOS, AND SIXES

About You	How Does This Affect Your Relationships?
You take responsibility for making situations better for others.	
You are intuitive about the feelings of others.	
You struggle with feelings of anxiety centered on what others think of you.	
You struggle to maintain your boundaries, which leaves you available to respond to the person or situation that is right in front of you.	
You focus more on *doing* and *feeling* than on *thinking*.	

THREES, SEVENS, AND EIGHTS

About You	How Does This Affect Your Relationships?
You give your time and attention to your own projects and ideas.	
You believe you can affect the world without being affected by it.	
You are quickly bored or impatient when more feeling types seem to endlessly share their feelings with you.	
You feel free to do whatever you want or need to do.	
You focus more on *doing* and *thinking* than on *feeling*.	

FOURS, FIVES, AND NINES	
About You	**How Does This Affect Your Relationships?**
You depend on your own strength to get you through.	
You are comfortable pulling back into yourself.	
You are accustomed to being focused inward.	
You often struggle to complete day-to-day tasks.	
You respond to stress by tuning out.	
You focus more on *thinking* and *feeling* than on *doing*.	

1. What have you learned about yourself in this session that is a surprise to you?

2. What were you surprised to learn about the others in your group?

3. Share some thoughts about obstacles you will face in learning to observe yourself nonjudgmentally. How might these obstacles relate to your Enneagram number?

4. Consider this guidance: "Practice allowing parts of your personality that don't serve you well to simply fall away." What's your initial response to this?

5. What one thing could you begin to work on that would have a positive effect on all of your relationships?

6. What relationship would you most like to strengthen? How might your own Enneagram number help you do that?

SESSION 2

WHAT WE WANT

*In my experience there are two things we have in common:
we all want to belong, and we all want our lives to have
meaning. But finding belonging and meaning are dependent
on our ability to build and maintain relationships—with
people who are like us, and often with those who are not.*

THE PATH BETWEEN US

Welcome back! This session we'll be focused on what motivates each number. We'll be revisiting some of the most important points about each number, but with a focus on the core motivation of each Enneagram type. Understanding what drives you, whether it's a desire to help others or to protect your own inner resources, brings you one step closer to improved relationships.

WHAT EACH NUMBER WANTS

Motivation is at the heart of the Enneagram. In fact, the key to understanding all Enneagram wisdom is to remember that a person's Enneagram number is determined by his or her motivation and not by behavior. People who seem to have similar goals, reactions, or behaviors can have entirely different motivations.

As you look at the following chart that names the core motivations for each Enneagram number, please keep in mind that the Enneagram is not static. At any given time, we may be healthy, average, or unhealthy in our responses. You have the opportunity in this session to note how your motivation is distorted when you are not doing well, perhaps because of stress, exhaustion, or other factors that keep you from responding appropriately.

In Healthy Range, Each Number Wants . . .	In Average or Unhealthy Range Each Number Might Want . . .
1 To make the world a better place	To feel better about themselves by being overly critical of others
2 To be needed	To feel valuable by creating relationships where others are dependent on them and then feel burdened by the responsibility
3 To be successful	To take shortcuts in their work, while walking away from people who don't agree with their agendas
4 To be understood and known while making meaningful connections with others	To manage their feelings about others by pushing them away and then pulling them back in
5 To be independent and seen as both capable and competent	To avoid contact with other people, isolating whenever possible while believing they can work out everything in their heads
6 To be connected to others while working toward goals that are for the common good	To give in to their struggle to trust themselves while feeling fearful and suspicious of others
7 To experience life and relationships to the fullest	To avoid slowing down in order to be faithful to their responsibilities or present to others
8 To lead others in doing their best at whatever is theirs to do, while fighting injustice wherever it exists	To demand that other people make up the difference that separates Eights from other numbers while ignoring how the others are affected by their behavior
9 Peace and harmony, and they are willing to mediate differences between people that cause separation and result in disconnection	To make choices that avoid conflict even when their involvement might be for the good of all involved

This chart offers some ideas of the differences between how we respond to life when we are in the healthy range and how we respond during times when we are struggling to make good decisions—both for ourselves and in our relationships. Keep these examples in mind as you respond to the following:

1. How are your relationships positively affected when you are in the healthy range, and how are they negatively affected when you are in the average to unhealthy range?

2. Share a time when your core motivation caused you to act or react in a way that was surprising to those you are in relationship with.

Examine one or two of your most valuable relationships and consider adjusting your motivation to something new and perhaps more relevant.

When we move too fast, when we don't think, and when we fail to consider feelings — ours and others' — we make decisions based on the things that motivate us in our personality. Essentially our personality is using us rather than the other way around. So, for the sake of relationships, it's always good to examine our motives for what we say or do because they can determine whether our behavior is in the healthy, average, or unhealthy range.

Intentionality is rare when we are caught up in the muchness and manyness of our lives. If we want to live our days in a better way, with more honorable motives, perhaps we need to spend time looking at the predictable, habitual, patterned motives that are connected to our Enneagram numbers.

Consider this example. Jane, Harry, and Tinesha are all medical residents training to become doctors. They all work at least a hundred hours a week diagnosing and caring for patients at the hospital. Although the three have similar lives, they are each very different:

Jane is training to be a doctor because, quite frankly, she is tired of being bossed around. She started her career as a nurse but found that doctors often ignored her ideas and even patients dismissed her suggestions. What Jane finds exhilarating about being a doctor is that she has a lot of responsibility and commands people's respect. People do complain, though, that she has "poor bedside manner" and can be overly blunt when speaking to patients.

> What we do is seldom more important than how we do it and why.

Harry is the most loved resident on the floor because he is always happy to help patients and other staff members. In fact, helping people is why he wanted to be a doctor in the first place, so he thrives on having a reputation for being generous with his time. A sensitive listener, he is often the first to notice what patients are *not* saying but are secretly feeling. He loves the way his job puts him in contact with people who need him, though he admits that his habit of working even more hours than the job requires puts his own health and core relationships in jeopardy. He just can't seem to say no to anyone.

Tinesha enjoys the expertise that comes with being a doctor, and she's proud of her title. She sometimes spends her free time studying about obscure conditions just because they're interesting. The human body never ceases to fascinate her. It's the constant interactions with people on the job that are draining—she always has to be "on" at the hospital, and just when she's becoming comfortable with one set of patients, they get discharged and she has a whole new crop of people to try to understand. So when work is over, Tinesha doesn't socialize with people from the hospital, preferring to curl up on the couch with her dog and a good book so she can recharge her batteries.

1. How are each of these people motivated differently?

2. How do their varying motivations translate into different behaviors?

3. Highlight a difference or similarity between what motivates you and what is identified as the motivation for Jane, Harry, or Tinesha.

EXPECTATIONS ARE RESENTMENTS WAITING TO HAPPEN

A common phrase heard among those in the recovery community is very helpful when studying the Enneagram: "expectations are resentments waiting to happen." All too often, we go through life with a host of desires that we may not have articulated to others, or even to ourselves. As we focus on motivation, it's important to ask ourselves this question: What do we expect, consciously or subconsciously, from other people?

Predictable Expectations from Each Number
1 That others have a desire to try to make things perfect
2 That others can sense and meet their needs
3 That others can set their feelings aside until a project is completed
4 That a commitment to authenticity is shared by most people
5 That others share and understand their need for physical and emotional space
6 That everyone is aware of the value of scanning the horizon for all that could go wrong
7 That reframing negative experiences into positive memories is both possible and a good thing
8 That people will be forthright in saying what's on their mind
9 That other people see at least two sides to most things

1. Name one or two things that you tend to want or expect from other people.

2. Name one or two things that those close to you seem to expect that don't come naturally to you.

3. How can the Enneagram help you in bridging the gap between expectations from others and your way of being in the world?

WHAT WE FEAR

Inability or unwillingness to appropriately deal with feelings is problematic. When others can't be honest . . . about what they feel and what they need, the delayed emotional responses are usually expressed as anger, shame, fear, or perhaps resentment, all of which are damaging to relationships.

THE PATH BETWEEN US

*O*ne of the most wonderful (and, let's be honest, one of the scariest) things about the Enneagram is that it tells us the truth about ourselves. In particular, it helps us understand some of the fears we have carried with us since childhood. For some numbers, their fears are obvious—like Sixes, whose anxiety is often verbalized, or Ones, who tend to see everything in terms of their own concern that it isn't good enough.

Our fears, whether we are aware of them or not, can have a significant impact on how we relate to others. In this session we will be discussing what each number wants to avoid in relationships and how our fears affect how we interact with the people we love.

FEARS AND RELATIONSHIPS

While we try not to be defined by our fears, we all have them. Fears are often associated with our Enneagram number. It is wise, in looking at how our personality type affects our lives, to explore our fears and the impact they might have on our relationships.

	What Each Number Fears	How Our Fears Affect Our Relationships
1	Believing they are flawed in some fundamental way, Ones are afraid of being wrong.	Ones avoid being judged as wrong or bad by seeking perfection in thought and word and deed. Unfortunately, as they work to "perfect" themselves they hold others to the same impossible standard they set for themselves.
2	Twos feel unworthy of being loved, so they are afraid to see themselves as loved and lovable.	When Twos operate from this place of believing they are unlovable, it's hard for them to receive and trust the love that is offered to them in relationships.
3	Threes believe they are loved for what they do and not for who they are.	By believing they are primarily loved for *doing*, Threes have a tendency to focus too much on work and accomplishments and too little on their relationships.
4	Fours are afraid they are "too much" in their desire to be seen and understood in relationships.	Fours have a tendency to over-explain themselves in connecting with other people who are important to them. It's a challenge to reassure a Four that you see them, understand them, and want to know them better.
5	Fives fear that they will not have adequate inner resources to meet the demands of relationships.	It is a big challenge when one person in a relationship needs significantly more downtime or time alone than the other.

6	Sixes have a lot of anxiety about many things that others seem unconcerned about.	Sixes require a lot of reassurance in relationships. Sometimes it is misunderstood as a lack of trust.
7	Sevens are afraid of being trapped in situations that are either boring or conflictual.	It's hard on relationships when Sevens overreact to routine or run from problems. They have to learn that every healthy relationship has at least two things in common: (1) Sometimes relationships are boring, *but not always*. (2) Conflict is inevitable, *but it can be worked out*.
8	Eights fear being controlled by others.	Eights are actually not interested in being in control of others. Their desire is to avoid being controlled *by* others. To that end, they have a tendency to operate independently. Healthy relationships thrive on interdependence.
9	Nines fear misunderstandings with others that might result in disconnection.	Nines tend to withhold their thoughts and preferences in an attempt to avoid conflict. Those who are in relationships with Nines want to know what they think, what they prefer, and how they feel. When they don't know, it feels like Nines are disengaged, and *that* is what can cause conflict.

Take some time to look at these fears, especially the one associated with your Enneagram number, and give some consideration to how they might affect relationships.

We all struggle to believe that we will be wanted, cared for, and understood by someone else because just under the surface, we all believe that there is something fundamentally wrong with us. We want to belong in a group or to another person and we want to believe that our presence has some kind of value. But it's a struggle when we have to manage so much anxiety about not being enough.

It will be good for your relationships if you can name and explore some of these fears, and perhaps others that are not listed, in the context of this group experience. The other people in your circle are afraid too—they're just afraid of different things and for different reasons.

Depending on the number of people in your group, break up into smaller groups of three or four to talk about your fears while answering the questions below:

1. Give an example of how the fear associated with your number in the chart has had a negative effect on your relationships.

2. How might it benefit your relationships if you could share one of the ways you think you are not enough with the other person?

3. When have you been able to deal with your own fears in a healthy way?

SELF-AWARENESS IS BOTH A GIFT AND A PRACTICE

Once people learn the Enneagram, they have a tendency to want to make changes in how they approach life—including how they relate to others. So they make a mental note or an actual list of the things they are not going to do going forward, or things they are going to do differently. It might include: "I'm going to stop helping so much," or "I'm going to be more social, go to more events, and make more connections," or even "I'm going to be more assertive about what I want and what I think."

Healthy relationships depend on our understanding that there are nine ways of seeing the world, nine ways of processing what we see, and nine ways of deciding how to proceed.

We're at the midpoint of our study together, so this is a good opportunity to think about a few of our core relationships (e.g., siblings, spouse, children, parents, friends). As you identify the positives in these relationships as well as the challenges, consider a change you could make to enhance these relationships.

Name:	Relationship:

Name some things about the relationship that are positive.

Name some things about the relationship that are challenging.

What changes could you make that would enhance this relationship?

Name:	Relationship:

Name some things about the relationship that are positive.

Name some things about the relationship that are challenging.

What changes could you make that would enhance this relationship?

1. In thinking about one of these relationships, what is a pattern that repeats itself over and over? How is it related to your Enneagram number (and the other person's number, if you know it)?

2. What could you do (or not do, or do differently) to break the cycle?

3. Sometimes our exchanges with those we love most become almost predictable—as if we're using the same script over and over. As you think about the outcomes that you want (or don't want) from these exchanges, consider what you could say different or differently. Are there questions you could ask in place of statements usually made? Maybe you need to articulate your fears or desires or hang-ups. Or maybe you need to change your tone so that what you say is received and understood. Brainstorm some examples of how you can "flip the script" in these verbal exchanges.

SESSION 4

WHAT WE OFFER

*Sometimes we get it right and other times we're
dead wrong. The good news is that with the
help of the Enneagram, we can all do better.*

THE PATH BETWEEN US

*E*very type on the Enneagram has
valuable gifts to offer in a relationship, gifts that may be exactly
what another person needs. In this session we'll explore some of
those gifts, focusing on the wonderful qualities embodied by those
we love as well as the qualities we ourselves may embody.

FIVE GREAT THINGS ABOUT YOU

There are terrific qualities associated with each number—and specifically with the people we care about—but we want to start out
by taking a look at our own very special qualities!

Think about times in your life when you have risen to the occasion in relationships, at work, or in other areas. What were you
able to contribute to a situation that no one else could? Take
some time by yourself to fill out the chart below, being as specific
as possible.

A time I felt great about myself	Guiding the antelope hunt @ Jaritas

A time I dealt well with adversity or setbacks	*chemo*
A time I expressed love and made someone feel very special	*Bringing Mom home from FL*
A time I accomplished something I never thought I could do	*Ropes course*
A time I was the exact friend that someone else needed	*Gerth's 50th Bday*
A time I made a plan and carried it out successfully	*CFI*

For some reason, it is difficult for most of us to name the things we like about ourselves and the things we do well.

In an effort to overcome that hesitation, please share one of the events from your chart with the people in your group.

1. What happened the time you accomplished something you thought you could never do, or the time you overcame a setback?

2. Which of the areas of the chart was the easiest to respond to? Why?

3. Did you get stuck on any of these questions? Why might those questions have been difficult for you?

Time I expressed love
Time I felt great about myself

Now think of what you know about the Enneagram numbers. Threes and Sevens, for example, have a natural advantage when it comes to reframing disappointment and overcoming setbacks, while Fours might have a built-in disadvantage there because they tend to have a hard time getting over the past. So that second question about dealing well with adversity might have been a breeze for Threes and Sevens but a stumbling block for Fours. On the other hand, Fours might have no problem at all thinking of a time when they made someone feel very special, so the third question might be right up Fours' alley; sensitive Fours want to feel special themselves and are often quite good at putting that into action for others.

> Our responses to life are determined by how we make sense of what we see, and how we decide to respond. It's different for every number.

1. Do you think that these areas of ease or challenge might have something to do with your Enneagram number?

2. Did you realize anything about your number when going through these questions?

3. What particular gifts does your number have to offer other people in relationship?

GREAT THINGS ABOUT EACH NUMBER

Now let's focus on the positive qualities of each number. There are five positive traits listed here, but rest assured that this list is just getting started! Each number has many, many gifts to offer, so this is the proverbial tip of the iceberg.

If possible, have someone who identifies with each particular number read that number's qualities aloud from "Five Terrific Qualities" (an Eight reads the qualities of Eights, etc.). After each is read, anyone else can mention other outstanding traits of that particular number that aren't on this list.

What other great things have you noticed about the Sevens, Threes, Ones, and so on, in your life?

Five TERRIFIC QUALITIES

1s
1 Sincerely want to make the world a better place
2 Have a strong moral compass
3 Are organized, reliable, and responsible
4 Are hard workers who think that if a job is worth doing, it's worth doing right
5 Have a superpower for pinpointing whatever is wrong in a situation

2s
1 Have an apparently endless supply of love for others
2 Perceive what someone else is feeling even before that person is aware
3 Place a high priority on close relationships
4 Are inherently compassionate toward the suffering of others
5 Give generously of their time and money

3s
1 Are successful and always seem to have an interesting project going on
2 Devote tremendous energy to getting the job done
3 Are positive, charming, and confident
4 Recover promptly from challenges or setbacks
5 Dare to dream big and make those dreams come true

4s
1 Are passionate, intense, and emotionally fierce
2 Almost always choose to be inclusive of everyone
3 Are creative, expressive, and drawn like a magnet to music and art

4 Trust their own intuition and visionary ideas

5 Don't avoid pain—their own or other people's

5s **1** Prefer a simple life and are not seduced by outward trappings of success

2 Can stay objective when other people's judgment is clouded by emotion

3 Value education, expertise, and reason

4 Are self-reliant and content being alone

5 Think carefully before making decisions

6s **1** Prioritize commitments to family, friends, and community

2 Like to be prepared for every scenario

3 Function well within a group or a team

4 Work hard and value duty and the common good

5 Aren't afraid to voice questions or doubts

7s **1** Can see the bright side of almost any situation

2 Are always looking forward to the next good or exciting thing

3 Don't get bogged down by worry or anxiety

4 Love learning and trying new things

5 Reframe any negative into a positive

8s **1** Have a remarkable amount of energy

2 Are assertive and direct—you always know where you stand with them

3 Can be loyal and protective of the people they love

4 Won't hesitate to take charge

5 Will often fight for the underdog

9s **1** Are peace loving and diplomatic

2 Go with the flow without getting upset if plans change

3 Are usually able to see both sides of an argument

4 Are patient and undemanding listeners

5 Appreciate beauty and nature

When I'm teaching I always include a short lecture about the importance of avoiding the temptation to assign numbers to other people. I close the speech with this: "While I am telling you not to assign numbers to other people, I know you are going to anyway. So I ask that you please leave room for the reality that you might be wrong."

You have been asked to answer questions and share stories about yourself during this study, and you have been exploring your relationships with others. So I'm sure you have assigned numbers to people you know and love. This is your opportunity to explore your thoughts about them in the context of Enneagram teaching. Think of three people you have a relationship with. Call to mind the things you admire most about them, times they have helped you when you needed it, and specific ways they have blessed your life. Take a few minutes on your own to fill out the chart below.

Name:

Qualities:

- ■
- ■
- ■

Name:

Qualities:

- ■
- ■
- ■

Name:

Qualities:

- ■

- ■

- ■

Share your list with the group as you discuss the following questions:

1. What specific traits or contributions do you see in your parents, spouse, siblings, or friends that you cherish?

2. How have those attributes made you feel loved or valued?

KEEPING EACH OTHER
FORGIVEN AND FREE

*We will always fall short in relationships, forever
working through disappointment with others. Even
though this is more difficult for some Enneagram
numbers than for others, we all need to give and
receive forgiveness. It's just part of the deal.*

THE PATH BETWEEN US

In the last session, we explored the
many gifts and graces of each number. But everything contains its
opposite, so in this session we'll be looking at how each number
misses the mark. We all have the desire to love well but sometimes
we fail, and when we do we often hurt those who are the closest to
us and who we care about the most.

First, we'll examine general patterns for each number, then we'll
get more personal by surveying our own relationship history—both
the ways we have been hurt and the ways we may have hurt others.
We may be walking into vulnerable, tender territory, so please be
kind and gracious with one another!

RELATIONSHIP LIMITATIONS FOR EACH NUMBER

Take some time to look over "Three Ways Each Number Limits
Relationships." If possible, read through the chart aloud and have
each reader be someone who is *not* that number, but who loves

someone of that number. For example, a Seven who is married to a Five might read the Five description, or a Two who loves and is worried about a Four child might read the Four description. The point of this is to show that even when we recognize hard truths about one another, we can do so in love.

Three WAYS EACH NUMBER LIMITS RELATIONSHIPS

1s 1 Pushing for perfection and constantly finding fault with others
     2 Taking responsibility for things that are not really in their stewardship and then resenting that responsibility
     3 Needing to be right all the time

2s 1 Overcommitting to people and causes until they burn out
     2 Assuming other people are needy and lost without them
     3 Becoming manipulative and controlling when they think they're losing someone's love

3s 1 Neglecting loved ones because of self-imposed pressure to succeed
     2 Playing the chameleon, so the real Three is buried beneath a series of façades
     3 Thinking of other people as extensions of themselves who reflect well or badly on them

4s 1 Being overly moody and self-absorbed
     2 Engaging in push-pull behavior as they draw you close out of fear that they will lose you and then push you away out of fear that they can't make it without you
     3 Believing that someone else can (and should) complete them

5s 1 Withdrawing from relationships because people's needs seem so draining
     2 Choose to make connections by participating rather than observing
     3 Being out of touch with their own emotions

6s 1 Doubting their relationships or partners
     2 Holding on to past hurts and disappointments
     3 Worrying so much that their anxiety alienates others

7s **1** Getting bored quickly and moving on so they can avoid negative experiences and emotions

2 Escaping reality through excess, entertainment, or addiction

3 Always wanting to get their own way

8s **1** Being unwilling to be vulnerable

2 Aggressively promoting their own agenda

3 Picking fights for no apparent reason

9s **1** Avoiding conflict to the point of ignoring serious problems

2 Sleepwalking through life and relationships

3 Rarely taking the initiative to begin, change, or end a relationship

Now consider your own experiences.

1. What rings true to you about the ways each type limits relationships?

2. Name ways that you limit relationships that are not on this list.

HOW WE HAVE BEEN HURT

While it can be painful to revisit times when you were wounded, it's valuable to do so with the added perspective of the Enneagram. Think about times from your past when other people have hurt you, either intentionally or unintentionally. Keep in mind that some numbers may have a more difficult time with this exercise than others. For example, Sevens and Threes tend not to dwell on the past, and Eights are often reluctant to remember any experiences where they felt weak or vulnerable.

Read through the following examples and then take some time to write down a few of your own.

Person	What Happened
Brother	Never calls or writes me, though he seems happy to hear from me when I get in touch. Disappeared completely when Mom got sick, and I had to make tough decisions about her care. If conflicts arise, says whatever he thinks will get people off his back, even if it's not actually true.
Boss	Working for her was like death by a thousand paper cuts. She had these subtle little digs all the time about the quality of my work. I don't think it ever occurred to her to pay anyone a compliment—it was always about how we could work better or harder or longer. One project I had worked so hard on and several other people were impressed by was sent back from her full of red changes. She also fixated on the fact that because it was going to require revisions, it would now be late. She gave me only a so-so performance review, which set back my timeline for promotion by a whole year.

Person	What Happened

As you look over your examples, answer the following questions:

1. Does the Enneagram help explain the experiences you wrote about in this exercise?

2. Are any of those old hurts still alive and well in your memory, or do you feel like you have been able to forgive?

3. How might your loved ones' actions have been shaped by the behaviors and attitudes that are typical of their Enneagram numbers?

HOW WE HAVE HURT OTHERS

There are three ways of meeting the world: feeling, thinking, and doing. The nine numbers of the Enneagram are divided among those three ways, known as triads. If possible, divide into groups by triad: a "Gut" group, a "Heart" group, and a "Head" group.

Center	The Gut Triad	The Heart Triad	The Head Triad
Numbers	8, 9, and 1	2, 3, and 4	5, 6, and 7
Struggles with	*Anger:* Eights act out their anger, Nines deny they experience it, and Ones internalize it	*Shame:* To escape shame, Twos serve others, Threes perform, and Fours cast themselves as victims	*Fear:* Fives battle fear by gaining knowledge, Sixes by aligning with (or challenging) authority, and Sevens by antici-pating a better future

In your triad group, look at the chart you filled out on page 34, but this time think about how *you* acted in those relationships. For example, in the hypothetical examples about the brother and the boss, a Three might realize that she was particularly frustrated by her brother's tendency to check out when their mother got sick because she had to play the role of the responsible child, making decisions all by herself, which is what everyone in the family expected of her. She might also see that in her relationship with the boss, she had a need for verbal affirmation and promotion at work, which her perfectionist boss seemed unable to provide. Rather than be thankful for her boss's attempts to improve her work, she was resentful because she was not put forward as a star.

> What we consider to be strengths in our twenties can easily become weaknesses in our thirties and forties and beyond if we aren't willing to engage in deep, self-reflective inner work.

As you look over your chart, discuss the following questions:

1. Do you think your own behavior contributed to or exacerbated the tensions?

2. How was your own behavior motivated by your Enneagram type?

3. In what ways have your behaviors limited your relationships?

4. Is there anything you might do differently if you could go back and make different choices, knowing what you now know about the Enneagram?

By listening to the people in your group you may find that some of your own relationship history now makes more sense. Even though the types are very different from one another, they are often attempting to deal with the same underlying issue, whether it's anger, shame, or fear.

WAYS TO HELP OURSELVES AND OTHERS

*Looking through the lens of the Enneagram
makes it possible to better understand ourselves
and others, increase our acceptance and
compassion, and navigate the paths between us.*

THE PATH BETWEEN US

*T*his week, we look at care and transformation in our own number as we pursue meaningful relationships. Wherever you are on the Enneagram, there are choices you can make that will make relationships easier and better—for yourself and for others.

COMPASSION FOR EVERY NUMBER

Every number struggles with something and experiences significant pain—they just struggle with different things. But what we learn from the Enneagram can help us grow in awareness. As we grow in awareness, our compassion and empathy increase, and we're able to extend grace to one another.

Take a look at "What to Remember About Loving Each Number." This chart exposes some of the hidden challenges for each number. If possible, read aloud the material *to* those of that number. In other words, a volunteer reads the Eight piece to a self-identified Eight, another volunteer reads the Nine description to a self-identified Nine, and so on. The idea is to acknowledge the particular struggle for each number so that each person can be lifted up and affirmed by the group.

What to Remember About Loving Each Number
1 Ones' criticism of others is a drop in the bucket compared to the criticism Ones regularly heap on themselves.
2 Twos focus on other people's needs so exclusively that they repress and do not recognize their own needs.
3 All the false images that Threes put forward in order to be seen as successful are exhausting for them to maintain.
4 Fours' depression and moody quest for a soulmate arise from the secret fear that they do not deserve to be loved.
5 Fives detach from relationships because every interaction demands a significant amount of their energy, not because they don't care.
6 Sixes' habit of scanning the horizon for threats is the outward manifestation of the worst-case scenario imaginings they live with 24/7.
7 Sevens may look carefree, but they flit from one activity or person to another because they're running from anxieties they don't know how to handle.
8 Deep down, Eights have a soft and tender side, but they feel they need to hide it so they won't get hurt.
9 Nines' tendency to discount their value in relationships reflects a deeper inclination to feel that nobody notices or cares about how they feel or what they think.

1. In what ways do you resonate with the statement about your number?

2. Is there anything else you could add to help others understand your number better? For example, a One might say, "Let me tell you about the inner critic in my head all day who

tells me I am fat, I am not working hard enough at my job, and I am neglecting my children even when I *do* work hard enough, and reminds me that I forgot my nephew's birthday again this year. I call that voice Myrtle. And she is with me—All. The. Time."

IDEAS FOR LOVING OTHERS BETTER

Sometimes we get things right in relationships—we say or do just the right thing that affirms and validates the one we love. But oftentimes we're a little misguided in our efforts. And other times we miss the mark entirely.

Read through the following chart as we explore ways to affirm, encourage, and strengthen those we love.

	A Thing to Say	A Thing *Not* to Say	A Thing to Do
1	"You are good enough already, just as you are."	"Why are you so uptight all the time?"	Don't leave them to do all the work, even if they do it well, and let them know they are loved despite the flaws they obsess about.
2	"Thank you for the ways you love and nurture me. I appreciate you."	"Can you stop being so emotional and try logic for just one second?"	Ask about the Two's feelings and problems. It's good when they are not always the people asking about yours.
3	"I love you for who you are, not what you accomplish."	"I'm surprised we went over budget. Your calculations usually come in as expected."	Encourage them to take a vacation and really disconnect from work in order to reconnect with their inner selves.

4	"You are really one-of-a-kind, and so special to me."	"Stop being such a drama queen. Cheer up already."	Remind them of beauty and goodness, and help them learn to love themselves—they are already enough. Nothing is missing.
5	"I appreciate your calm and your thought-fulness."	"Why are you always so quiet and secretive?"	Try not to blindside them with new situations or ask them to make decisions without ample time to reflect.
6	"I'm not going anywhere. I am here for you."	"Aaaaaaugh, please stop with all the worrying."	Help them have confidence in their own abilities, especially their ability to make decisions. Be trustworthy and do what you say you will do.
7	"Life is always more interesting with you here."	"Am I not enough for you? Is our life not enough?"	Give them freedom and resist the urge to tell them what to do. At the same time, encourage them to remember that less is more.
8	"I appreciate your strength, but I am a safe person for you to be vulnerable with."	"Who decided you should be in charge?"	Stand your ground and don't be cowed by them. Remind them that moderation is a virtue.
9	"Your opinion matters to me. I want to hear it."	"Are you ever going to get around to doing what you said you would do?"	When they're facing a decision, you might help them narrow down the options or make a list of pros and cons—but then walk away. Do not make the decision for them, no matter how slow they are.

Thinking back to what we've learned about each number's fears can give us some clues about how to proceed (e.g., reassure a Three that your future love is not based on their past performance; give a Five space to breathe and time alone; let a Nine make decisions; give a One a good deal of verbal affirmation).

Discuss the following questions together:

1. Give an example of a time when someone else said just the right thing to you. How did you respond?

2. Have you ever tried to say something like what's on this chart to a loved one? What was their response?

3. Identify one thing on this list that you can put into action right away in a core relationship.

CARE AND TRANSFORMATION OF YOUR NUMBER

For this final conversation, read through the chart below as a group.

For Each Number, Know That It's Okay to . . .	Five Ideas for Each Number for Growth in Relationships
1 Make mistakes	1. Try giving your inner critic a name. Acknowledge faithful running commentary, and then go on with your day. 2. Be sparing about telling the people you love what they should do. Instead, try focusing on the things they're doing right. 3. Accept that you're wrong sometimes, and that's okay. You will make mistakes. 4. Take breaks and have some fun! The work will still be there later. 5. Do something nice for yourself today, just because.

2	Have limits	1. Spend some time alone today doing something you enjoy, apart from other people.
		2. The next time you're tempted to jump in, try imagining that most of the people around you are actually doing just fine without your help.
		3. When you give to others, remind yourself that you aren't expecting something in return. (Repeat as necessary.)
		4. Practice being direct about your own wants and needs, rather than hoping other people will just pick up those vibes by osmosis.
		5. Set some boundaries around the time and attention you're willing to provide other people.
3	Be yourself	1. Try putting relationships before work at least once a day. Your loved ones will thank you for it.
		2. Appreciate the success you already have without always looking ahead to the next hoop you plan to jump through.
		3. Allow something to be posted on social media that shows you in a negative light, like an unflattering photograph or story. (And don't try to sell it as a positive.)
		4. Ask yourself regularly what you are feeling. The results may surprise you.
		5. Try a regular practice of sitting in silence for ten minutes a day.
4	Be ordinary	1. Catch yourself when you begin to envy other people's happiness, relationships, or ease in the world.
		2. Channel your deep feelings about suffering toward others; you are one of the best people around to empathize with their pain.
		3. Be grateful for the relationships you have right now, rather than dreaming of ideal ones that do not exist.
		4. Find ways every day to express your creativity.
		5. Understand that your intense emotions may be overwhelming to others, and try to dial down that intensity when you're communicating with them.

5	Love whole-heartedly	1. Try actually explaining your social limitations to the people you care about and letting them in on the plan: "I'll come to the party for one hour, and then I will probably go home. But my leaving early is not about you." 2. Risk giving up a bit of your privacy so you can have closer relationships. 3. Indulge yourself in a creature comfort or two. 4. Be careful that you are not dismissing your loved ones' ideas, thoughts, or offers of help. 5. When other people talk about their feelings, don't immediately analyze those feelings as thoughts (or as problems to solve). Aim to connect on a heart level.
6	Trust yourself	1. Initiate an adventure by yourself and for yourself, and don't plan the life out of it. 2. Make a choice or decision without second-guessing yourself afterward. 3. Have a "happy place" you can go to in your mind when the worries you feel threaten to overwhelm you. 4. Be careful not to deal with your anxieties by working too much. 5. Give yourself a set amount of time—say, five minutes—to catastrophize. Then try to set the worst-case scenario aside.
7	Face pain	1. Resist the urge to make light of serious situations or to flee other people's pain. Just sit with them a while. 2. Finish a project before you start the next one. 3. Try to stay in the moment where you are and present with the people around you. 4. At least once a day, let someone else have their way, and do not pout about it. 5. Remember that oftentimes less is more.

8	Be vulnerable	1. Be careful about the words you use. You may think you're just "telling it like it is," but others may hear it as harsh or intimidating.
		2. Tell people you love them! It's not a sign of weakness.
		3. Try this week to pick fights only with other Eights. They will actually enjoy it. Others will enjoy the break from your signature jousting.
		4. Practice consciously letting go of your need for control of a group or situation.
		5. Own up to a mistake today rather than defaulting to loudly spreading blame elsewhere.
9	Say no	1. Add some structure to your routine every day, making a brief list of the most important things you need to do. Then actually do them.
		2. Speak up for yourself! Your voice is important and valuable.
		3. Stay aware of the times you want to zone out. Are you using TV, food, or excessive sleep to avoid conflict?
		4. Express your anger clearly when you feel it—don't save it up so that you explode like a volcano at an unexpected time.
		5. Practice saying no to something every day. Just try it.

If possible, join up with two or three other people of your choosing. Share what you have learned as you answer the following questions:

1. Have you tried any of these ideas for growth in the past? What was the result?

2. Which of these ideas seem to be the most helpful?

3. What other ideas for growth have worked for you that are not on this list?

Remember that you can never change how you see. All you can do is change *what you do* with how you see, and the Enneagram can help you take those steps. Congratulations on reaching the finish line here, and best wishes in your further journey of self-discovery through the Enneagram.

GUIDANCE FOR LEADERS

Although it's helpful to have read books about the Enneagram and be familiar with the different types, it is definitely not a requirement to lead this group. In fact, because your role is to guide conversations, not to teach, don't worry if you are fairly new to the Enneagram. This guide will work for those who know even just a little about the Enneagram. What's most important is that you keep the tone positive, the group focused, and the discussion helpful, and make space for all participants to contribute to the conversation.

A FEW TIPS

FACILITY: You will want a room that is large enough to accommodate your group's size, which can vary from group to group (and even sometimes from session to session). For a larger group, it's particularly helpful to have a space that can accommodate breaking off into pairs or trios when necessary.

NAMETAGS: If your group is large, you may wish to have nametags that participants can use from session to session. If so, have the nametags printed and ready to go in advance, with a few blank ones for drop-ins.

PAPER AND PENS: Have blank sheets of paper and pens available each session. If you are super-organized and have a budget, it would be great if you also gave each participant a folder or notebook of some kind, but you could also just encourage them to bring their own.

TIME: Each session is designed to last about ninety minutes total, but don't feel legalistic about the suggested time allotted for each section (are you listening, Ones?). Each group is different, so different elements will resonate more or less from session to session. Keep in mind that you don't have to complete an entire session in a single gathering, so wherever you are after ninety minutes is a good place to stop. You can just pick up there the next time.

GATHERING: Beginnings are important, so don't try to just dive right into the curriculum. We've offered a few suggestions, but the makeup of your group will determine how you want to start each session off—whether it's a prayer, a song, an icebreaker question, or something else.

CLOSING: You'll want to honor everyone's time, so reserve those last five minutes to bring everyone back together before dismissing. At that point you can forecast the topic for the next session, issue a challenge from the session, make important announcements, or just point everyone toward the refreshments.

TAKE SOME RISKS: One of your tasks as a leader is to moderate and make sure that everyone who wants to participate has the opportunity. That means you need to keep any one person (including yourself) from dominating the conversation. However, as a leader you will often have the opportunity to set the tone of the conversation. And if you are willing to be vulnerable—especially when you sense that the discussion has stayed in the shallow end—you will help your group grow.

REFRESHMENTS (OPTIONAL): If you would like to have a time of fellowship and food before or after each session, and the building that hosts your group has no objections, consider passing a sign-up sheet the first session and having people volunteer for a session when they can bring a snack to share.

SESSION 1: THE BEST PART OF YOU IS THE WORST PART OF YOU

GATHERING (20 MINUTES): If possible, have participants gather their chairs in a circle so that everyone can see and hear one another. After welcoming everyone and introducing yourself, give a brief opening prayer if that is comfortable for your group, or designate someone else to do so. If you don't wish to come up with your own invocation, you might consider these words from the Episcopal Book of Common Prayer: "Almighty God, to you all hearts are open, all desires known, and from you no secrets are hid: Cleanse the thoughts of our hearts by the inspiration of your Holy Spirit, that we may perfectly love you, and worthily magnify your holy Name; through Christ our Lord. Amen."

Review the ground rules on page 2 and see if there are any questions or additional needs that participants have for your time together.

Then invite participants to go around the room and introduce themselves, sharing the following three details:

- first name
- hometown
- a strength or characteristic they like about themselves

This needs to proceed quickly—there will be plenty of time for deeper sharing later.

STRENGTHS AND WEAKNESSES OF OUR NUMBERS (30 MINUTES): Review "Some of the Best and Worst of Us" together. Then, if possible, break into groups of three to discuss where each person thinks they fall on the Enneagram and in what ways their number's strength may also be their weakness. But first highlight the counsel about not attempting to assign numbers to each other—doing so robs other people of the joy of their own journey. Each person should take about seven or eight minutes total.

THE CHALLENGE OF CHANGE (35 MINUTES): Remind your group that we *all* have challenges in relationships. In this activity, we are attempting to recognize the different challenges that we each encounter. The charts are grouped by stances. For more information, see page 11 of *The Path Between Us*. If possible, after reading the entire section with the large group, break into groups of three to discuss the questions.

CLOSING (5 MINUTES): Five minutes before the end of the session, begin to wrap up the discussion. Tell everyone that next session you will be exploring what each number wants or what motivates each number. If they have a chance, participants should look over the relevant material from *The Path Between Us*, which is in the opening section of each chapter (e.g., "The World of Fours").

SESSION 2: WHAT WE WANT

GATHERING (5 MINUTES): Invite someone to open with prayer, read the invocation from the Book of Common Prayer suggested last session, or use some other method of bringing the group together to begin your time.

WHAT EACH NUMBER WANTS (40 MINUTES): In the large group, sitting in a circle if space allows, explain that this session will focus on what motivates each number.

First, read through the chart of motivations (healthy and unhealthy range). Then allow about fifteen to twenty minutes to use the chart as the group addresses the discussion questions. Essentially, participants are asked to reflect on the idea that "the best part of you is the worst part of you." These realizations can be painful for some people. Please remind them that there's no right or wrong number on the Enneagram; every one of the nine types has its own gifts and its own obstacles.

Then read through the examples of Jane, Harry, and Tinesha. As you discuss the questions, remind the group to focus on *motivations* rather than try to assign numbers to these three individuals.

EXPECTATIONS ARE RESENTMENTS WAITING TO HAPPEN (40 MINUTES): Encourage the group to explore the chart about expectations and discuss what they tend to want from other people and what others seem to want from them.

CLOSING (5 MINUTES): Tell everyone that next session they will be exploring what each number fears. If they have a chance, they can look over the relevant material from *The Path Between Us,* the fear sections of each chapter.

SESSION 3: WHAT WE FEAR

GATHERING (5 MINUTES): Invite someone to open with prayer, read the invocation from the Book of Common Prayer suggested in session one, or use some other method of bringing the group together to begin your time.

FEARS AND RELATIONSHIPS (40 MINUTES): Explain that two of the six sessions address fairly negative topics: sessions three and five. But just as the Enneagram itself reminds us that we have both strengths and weaknesses, they're sandwiched by more positive sessions. In other words, even though this week might be difficult for some, encourage them to persevere!

This is a good opportunity to acknowledge that it can be frightening to talk about our fears with other people—and probably more frightening for some Enneagram types than others. This is also a good opportunity to remind everyone that what is said in the group stays in the group, and that we are not here to judge one another or to give advice—we're just here to listen to others and to share our own discoveries.

Review the chart about what each number fears and how those fears may affect our relationships. Ask for volunteers to read each number's description aloud. This should ideally take just a few minutes, but if you sense that people are ready to say more about whether something about their number resonates with their own experience, be flexible and allow them to speak about that.

If possible, have participants break into small groups of their choosing (though you might encourage them to join with two or three people they do not already know well) to respond to the discussion questions.

SELF-AWARENESS IS BOTH A GIFT AND A PRACTICE (40 MINUTES): Since the end of this session marks the halfway point for this study, this activity is intended to help the group recalibrate. Using what they've learned about themselves and their knowledge of the Enneagram, they'll have the opportunity to consider some changes—doing or saying things different or differently—that will make a positive impact on their relationships.

CLOSING (5 MINUTES): Tell everyone that next session they will be exploring what each number has to offer others in relationships. They will have probably already read the first few sections of each chapter in *The Path Between Us,* but they might want to review that material if they have time, paying special attention to what is unique and wonderful about each number.

SESSION 4: WHAT WE OFFER

GATHERING (5 MINUTES): Invite someone to open with prayer, read the invocation from the Book of Common Prayer suggested in session one, or use some other method of bringing the group together to begin your time.

Five Great Things About You (40 minutes): It's time to accentuate the positive! Allow participants about ten minutes to fill out the chart identifying times in their lives when they have risen to the occasion in relationships, at work, or in other areas (they may need writing paper for more space). Then invite participants to gather with two or three people as they review their charts and answer the discussion questions.

Great Things About Each Number (40 minutes): In the large group, read aloud "Five Terrific Qualities." If possible, have someone who identifies with each particular number read that number's qualities aloud to the whole group. After each number, invite people to mention other outstanding traits they've noticed about that particular number that aren't on this list.

Have participants take about ten minutes to fill out the chart in their study guide with some of the most admirable qualities of three people they love. Then bring the large group back together to share some of those observations as they respond to the discussion questions.

Closing (5 minutes): Tell everyone that next session they will be exploring how each number might limit relationships. The relevant materials in each chapter in *The Path Between Us* are the sections "Stress and Security" and "Limitations in Relationships." If they would like to read those in advance of the session, it would be helpful, but as always it is not a requirement.

SESSION 5: KEEPING EACH OTHER FORGIVEN AND FREE

Gathering (10 minutes): Because the group is now more familiar with one another, you might want to have a slightly longer opening exercise with a few minutes set aside for silent meditation.

This is a chance for participants to settle into a more reflective mode of being, opening themselves to any epiphanies that may occur during the session. Some types find that this kind of meditation comes fairly naturally, such as Nines (who rarely seem impatient that there is somewhere else they'd rather be), Fours (who are keenly interested in accessing the deepest parts of themselves), and Fives (who are more comfortable with solitude and silence than anyone else on the Enneagram). Others—such as Ones and Threes, who find much of their value in productivity—might consider a few minutes of silent meditation to be a struggle or even a waste of time. Reassure participants that there is grace here. If their minds wander, they should not scold themselves about it. That's just part of the process.

Ask participants to sit comfortably in their chairs with both feet resting on the floor and close their eyes. Depending on your group, you can either read a passage from the Bible or just opt for silent reflection. If your group is comfortable with a reading from the Bible, here is a passage from the Gospel of Matthew that would be good fodder for the silent reflection in this session.

> Why do you look at the speck of sawdust in your brother's eye and pay no attention to the plank in your own eye? How can you say to your brother, "Let me take the speck out of your eye," when all the time there is a plank in your own eye? You hypocrite, first take the plank out of your own eye, and then you will see clearly to remove the speck from your brother's eye. (Matthew 7:3-5)

Allow five or six minutes of silence, which does not sound like much but can feel like an eternity to people who are not used to it. When the time is up, gently invite everyone to open their eyes and, if they need to, move around a bit before beginning the discussion.

RELATIONSHIP LIMITATIONS FOR EACH NUMBER (20 MINUTES): Remind the group that this is one of the two sessions where we will be looking at each number's potential downsides—in this case, possible patterns that each type has for limiting relationships and hurting those closest to us. As with the session on fear (session three), this can be a hard week for some people—it's often difficult to hear uncomfortable truths about ourselves. Be as encouraging and matter-of-fact about this as you can, and remind the group that *every* type engages in behavioral patterns that limit relationships.

In your large group, read through "Three Ways Each Number Limits Relationships." Ask that each reader be someone who is *not* of that number themselves, but who loves someone of that number. The point of this is to show participants that even when they recognize hard truths about one another, they can do so in love. Use this sidebar as you respond to the discussion questions.

HOW WE HAVE BEEN HURT (30 MINUTES): Allow individuals ten to fifteen minutes to fill out the chart identifying wounding events from their past. Encourage them to choose a few experiences in their core relationships and write about those. Then bring the group back together to examine what they wrote as they respond to the discussion questions.

HOW WE HAVE HURT OTHERS (25 MINUTES): In this section we're going to break into small groups by triad, which we have not done before. When we hear how other people in our triad have behaved in relationships, more of our own relationship history may begin to make sense to us. Even though the numbers in each triad are very different from one another, they are often attempting to deal with the same underlying issue, whether it's anger (Eights, Nines, and Ones), shame (Twos, Threes, and Fours), or fear (Fives,

Sixes, and Sevens). You can look at pages 8 and 9 of *The Path Between Us* for more information.

Encourage participants to use the charts they just filled out but to reflect primarily on their own behavior as they address the discussion questions. We want to better understand how the default behaviors we gravitate toward, particularly in times of stress, have undermined our goal to have harmonious, healthy relationships with others.

CLOSING (5 MINUTES): Tell everyone that next session, the final session, they will be exploring care and transformation in their own numbers as they pursue meaningful relationships. The relevant materials in *The Path Between Us* are the lists at the end of each chapter on ways to improve relationships. If participants would like to read those in advance of the session, it would be helpful, but as always it is not a requirement.

SESSION 6: WAYS TO HELP OURSELVES AND OTHERS

GATHERING (10 MINUTES): This final session will again offer the opportunity for a slightly longer opening exercise with a few minutes set aside for silent meditation. Please reassure participants that there is grace here: if their minds wander, they should not scold themselves about it. That's just part of the process.

Ask participants to sit comfortably in their chairs with both feet resting on the floor and close their eyes. Depending on your group, you can either read a passage from the Bible or just opt for silent reflection. If your group is comfortable with reading the Bible, here is a short passage from 1 Peter that would be good for the silent reflection in this session.

> Each of you should use whatever gift you have received to serve others, as faithful stewards of God's grace in its various forms. (1 Peter 4:10)

Allow six or seven minutes of silence. When the time is up, gently invite everyone to open their eyes and, if they need to, move around a bit before beginning the discussion.

COMPASSION FOR EVERY NUMBER (20 MINUTES): Explain that the first step toward helping ourselves and others through the Enneagram is awareness, and that awareness increases our compassion for one another.

Read through "What to Remember About Loving Each Number." Ideally, you want to direct your reading about each number *to* those of that number (a volunteer reads the Eight piece to a self-identified Eight, another volunteer reads the Nine description to a self-identified Nine, etc.).

Then give the group the opportunity to respond to the discussion questions in order to increase our understanding and awareness of each number.

IDEAS FOR LOVING OTHERS BETTER (25 MINUTES): Keeping the large group together, review the chart about "a thing to say," "a thing *not* to say," and "a thing to do." You may also want to review the material from session three on what each number fears most as you respond to the discussion questions.

CARE AND TRANSFORMATION OF YOUR NUMBER (30 MINUTES): As a large group, read through the chart together. If possible, split into smaller groups of three or four to respond to the discussion questions. Encourage participants to examine each number in the chart as they identify ideas for growth that may be helpful in their relationships.

CLOSING (5 MINUTES): Remind participants that they can never change how they see. All they can do is change what they do with what they see, and the Enneagram can help them take those steps.

Express your hope that they will continue their journey of self-discovery through the Enneagram, and congratulate them on reaching the end of this course!

ALSO AVAILABLE

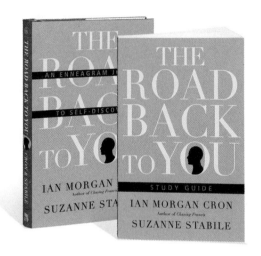

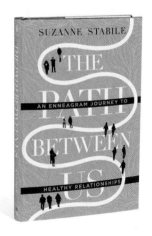

LIFE IN THE TRINITY
MINISTRY

Drawing on timeless wisdom and the Living Word, Life in the Trinity Ministry is a community serving the Triune God and our brothers and sisters through study dedicated to encouraging self-knowledge and fostering spiritual maturity.

What does the Lord require of you but to do justice, and to love kindness, and to walk humbly with your God? Micah 6:8

The Enneagram: Know Your Number
Suzanne Stabile

The Enneagram: Wings, Stress and Security
Suzanne Stabile

The Aggressive Stance, The Dependent Stance,
and *The Withdrawing Stance*
Suzanne Stabile

The Enneagram Journey DVD Curriculum
and *Participant's Guide*
Suzanne Stabile

Centering Prayer
Reverend Joseph Stabile

For more information about Suzanne or any of these resources, go to lifeinthetrinityministry.com.